PIERO VENTURA'S
BOOK OF

Parade in Copenhagen, Denmark

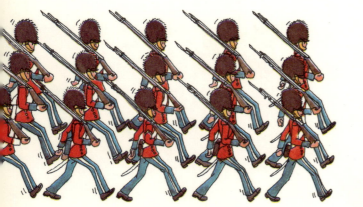

CiTiES

Random House 🏠 New York

Library of Congress Cataloging in Publication Data
Ventura, Piero.   Piero Ventura's Book of cities.   SUMMARY: Text and illustrations present some of the outstanding features of the world's most famous cities.
1. Cities and towns. [1. Cities and towns] I. Title. II. Title: Book of cities. G140.V36   301.36'3   74-4927   ISBN 0-394-82744-9   ISBN 0-394-92744-3 lib. bdg.
Manufactured in the United States of America   1 2 3 4 5 6 7 8 9 0

To my three sons—
Marco and the twins, Paolo and Andrea.

If they had not asked me so many questions
about how people lived in other cities around
the world, I might never have written and
illustrated this book.

Author's Note

In recreating scenes from cities that I have visited and tried to describe to my sons in words and sketches, I should like to ask a certain artist's license. These illustrations are not exact reproductions—a camera could do that better than I! They are instead an attempt to combine the special elements and colorful impressions that made each city a unique experience for me.

I hope I will be forgiven if I have omitted the reader's own city. It may very well be at the top of my next itinerary.

Piero Ventura

Milan, Italy

Because cities are so crowded, transportation is usually a real problem. How can so many people get to work? (Often a person lives many miles from the place where he works.) How can enough supplies and food be brought into the city every day?

City streets are always full of traffic. Cars, trucks, buses, and taxicabs fight for space. Trains, boats, and planes are constantly carrying people in and out of the city.

In an effort to get some of the traffic off the streets, more and more cities have introduced underground trains or subways. And usually there are special highways to move cars over and around cities without their getting into the crowded streets.

Many cities are located at busy ports where ocean-going freighters and passenger ships can easily dock. Others are on rivers and canals, so boats and flat-bottomed barges can provide transportation in and out of the city. And almost always cities are at the center of a complex system of railways.

Cities with good transportation facilities are the ones that become big.

Cars and trucks, buses and taxis, bicycles and motorbikes jam the streets of London. One of the most crowded places in the city is called Piccadilly Circus. (In England a "circus" is a circle or square where a number of streets meet.) At Piccadilly, six of London's busiest streets come together around a statue of Eros, the Greek god of love. He seems to float over the intersection with his drawn bow.

At Piccadilly you never have to look far to find one of London's famous bright red double-decker buses. London buses are different from those of most other cities. They have an upstairs and a downstairs. Narrow, winding stairs lead to the upper deck. It is not easy to climb up if the bus is going fast, but once you reach the top you have a wonderful view. You can look down on office workers, store windows, and pedestrians.

There are often big traffic jams like this at Piccadilly Circus. But they aren't always caused by a family of dachshunds trying to get across the street. However, in London people love their pets so much that a policeman thinks nothing of stopping traffic so a family of dogs can cross the road safely.

City buses run on top of the ground, but city trains are likely to travel below the ground. New York City has miles and miles of subways running underground. Express trains often run on tracks below the local trains. (And at this stop, a different subway line crosses between the local and the express.) Moving stairways called escalators carry people from one level to another. Without ever going aboveground, a passenger can shop in a department store, stop for a hot dog, or buy a bunch of flowers to take home. When trains pull in, people rush to get on and off, bumping into each other, dropping papers, losing money. To get onto the subway platform, you have to put a token in the turnstile. You buy tokens at a change booth. Sometimes young graffiti artists paint their names in bright colors on subway cars.

There are also "department stores" that are outdoors. You will find many of these in Baghdad, the colorful capital of Iraq, in the Middle East. Here, for hundreds of years, merchants have gathered to display their wares in outdoor markets. They come into the center of the city with their amazing assortment of merchandise packed on camels and donkeys. You can find almost anything you want if you look hard enough—clothing, jewelry, carpets; even an old sewing machine or a clothes dryer. Nobody expects you to pay the asking price. You have to bargain. And you can look at an article as long as you like. In fact, you can even try it out. A lot of the things for sale may be worthless, but a shrewd shopper can often find some real bargains and wonderful curiosities. If you get bored with shopping, there are usually jugglers, fire eaters, or snake charmers to entertain you.

This is the harbor at Hamburg, West Germany, one of the largest seaports in Europe. Hamburg is a perfect port because it is located on two lakes and two rivers, as well as a whole system of canals. One of the rivers, the Elbe, provides it with easy access to the North Sea. It is also one of the leading railroad centers in West Germany.

The port section of a city has a life all its own. It has a special traffic system, and the dockside workers have their own way of talking and doing things. Tugboats lead the big freighters into the harbor. Tall cranes unload all the goods that are packed into these floating storehouses, and fill them up again with new freight for their next stop. There are special police to supervise the harbor, and all kinds of freight cars and barges to carry goods to and from the busy waterfront.